The

D1651860

They said, "Jesus must be a very special man.
Even the wind and the water do what Jesus says."

Jesus' friends were very surprised.

The storm stopped.

Then Jesus got up.
He spoke to the wind and the water.

Jesus said,
"Why are you frightened?
You should trust me."

"Lord, save us," they said.
"The boat will sink
and we will all die."

Jesus' friends woke him up.

But Jesus was still asleep.

The wind blew
and the water came into the boat.

Suddenly a storm started.

Jesus went to sleep.

They sailed off
to the other side
of the big lake.

Jesus got into a boat.
His friends got in too.

Jesus and the Storm

What the Bible Tells Us Series

The text of these books has been rewritten
on the basis of Today's English Version,
keeping as much of the New Testament stories
as can be understood by the intended readers.

Illustrations by Kees de Kort

First United States Paperback Edition 1979

Original Dutch Version © 1967
Netherlands Bible Society, Hilversum

English Text © 1977
British and Foreign Bible Society

International Standard Book No. 0-8066-1683-0

Manufactured in the United States of America

P 246

AUGSBURG Publishing House
Minneapolis, Minnesota

EMORY UNITED METHODIST CHURCH

EMORY UNITED METHODIST CHURCH

Jesus and the Storm

Jesus Goes Away